Politics Today

Trade Unions and Pressure Groups

Stewart Ross

 **Politics Today**

The Alliance Parties
The Cabinet and Government
The Conservative Party
Elections
The European Parliament
The House of Commons
The House of Lords
The Labour Party
Local Government
The Monarchy
The Prime Minister
Trade Unions and Pressure Groups

Editor: Francesca Motisi

First Published in 1987 by
Wayland (Publishers) Ltd
61 Western Road, Hove
East Sussex BN3 1JD

© Copyright 1987 Wayland (Publishers) Ltd

British Library Cataloguing in Publication Data
Ross, Stewart
  Trade Unions and Pressure Groups. – (Politics today)
  1. Trade-unions – Great Britain – Political activity – Juvenile
  literature 2. Great Britain – Politics and government – 1979
  – Juvenile literature 3. Pressure groups – Great Britain – Juvenile
  literature 4. Great Britain – Politics and government – 1981
  – Juvenile literature
  I. Title
  322'.2'0941   HD8395

  ISBN 1 85210 290 X

Photoset by
Kalligraphics Ltd, Redhill, Surrey
Printed in Italy by
G. Canale & C.S.p.A., Turin
Bound in the UK by
The Bath Press, Avon

Front Cover: *A NUT
demonstration for more pay,
London.*

Contents

Representative Government

A true democracy is a system of government which involves all adults in each government decision. This is impossible in a large country like Britain, so we elect representatives to govern on our behalf. These representatives, whom we choose at general elections, form the government. This is known as a representative democracy. Under the British system the life of a government can be anything up to five years.

If our democracy is to remain effective, it is important for the government to keep in touch with the people it governs between elections. There are many ways in which this can happen. Opinion polls offer some indication of the nation's thinking. Members of Parliament gather local opinion by meeting their constituents and reading their letters. Television and the newspapers also

Opinion polls help the government keep in touch with the people between elections.

reflect the climate of opinion. Pressure groups are another way of keeping the government in touch with the people.

These groups consist of people who share a common aim or interest, and who try to influence local or central government to further their cause. They vary in size from the mighty Transport and General Workers' Union to a branch of the Ramblers' Association, whose prime interest might be to keep open a local footpath.

It is important in a democracy that pressure groups are allowed to express their opinions and carry out their activities without interference. But as well as being useful, pressure groups can sometimes give rise to problems. What tactics should they be allowed to use to get their point of view across? And should there be democratic controls over the very large groups such as the unions, which can challenge the authority of the elected government itself?

Anyone can join a pressure group. These young conservationists are from Harrogate, in Yorkshire. Like members of Greenpeace and Friends of the Earth, they are working to save our environment.

5

Parties and Pressure Groups

At first glance, pressure groups and political parties appear quite similar. They are both concerned with influencing people and decisions. They both also rely on their members' subscriptions for financial support, and allow their members to choose leaders to represent them. But here the similarity ends. Pressure groups and political parties differ in three important ways.

Firstly, pressure groups try to influence the government but not to form it. The Labour Party, for example, exists to try to form a Labour government. The National Union of Mineworkers, on the other hand, while contributing money to Labour Party funds, and even sponsoring Labour parliamentary candidates, does not seek to help its membership by forming a separate group in Parliament or on the local council.

The Labour Party exists to try to form a Labour government whereas pressure groups like the unions are concerned mainly with the interests of their members. Here Neil Kinnock, leader of the Labour Party is joined by his wife Glenys to receive a standing ovation at the 1984 conference.

A second difference is that political parties try to appeal to all people, because they need as many votes as possible to win elections. Pressure groups are concerned only with the interests of their members. Finally, most pressure group members are not always primarily concerned with politics. Members of the National Farmers' Union, for example, are interested in new varieties of wheat as well as more political issues, such as EEC farm subsidies. Political parties, however, are wholly concerned with the exercise of political power.

'Pressure group' is a very general term. Most observers distinguish between 'cause' groups and 'interest' groups. The former try to further a particular cause. One of the best-known of these groups is the Campaign for Nuclear Disarmament (CND). Interest groups exist to look after the interests of a particular group of citizens. By far the most prominent and successful among this group, over the last century or so, have been the trade unions.

Arthur Scargill, chairman of the NUM (National Union of Mineworkers) marches through London with miners' wives. They were protesting against pit closures in 1984.

7

Early Trade Unions

Throughout history, people in the same trade have joined together for mutual benefit. In the Middle Ages master craftsmen formed guilds to protect their standards and prices, but unions of ordinary working people were rare, and frowned upon by the authorities. By the late eighteenth century the situation began to change. The Industrial Revolution brought together large numbers of workers in terrible conditions, while the French Revolution gave birth to new radical ideas of fairness and equality in society.

Faced with the possibility of widespread working-class unrest at a time when the country was at war with France, Parliament passed two Combination Acts (1799 and 1800). These made trade unions and strikes illegal, and were enforced by harsh penalties. After the war a successful

Craftsmen, like these masons, formed guilds in the Middle Ages, to maintain standards and protect their prices.

ESTABLISHED
1887.
HULL SEAMENS & MARINE FIREMENS
AMALGAMATED ASSOCIATION
GOD HELPS THOSE WHO HELP THEMSELVES

This is a banner of one of the first trade unions. By the 1880s Britain had a successful union movement with well over one million members.

campaign was mounted to repeal the Combination Acts. A new Combination Act (1825) allowed a form of unionism but made strikes of doubtful legality. For a while trade unions flourished, reaching a peak with Robert Owen's Grand National Consolidated Trade Union (1834). But the GNCTU soon folded and, without the right to withhold their labour, nineteenth century unions were restricted to being scarcely more than friendly societies.

The 'New Model' unions, comprising mainly of law-abiding skilled workers, gradually won a reduction of the laws restricting their activities. This resulted in the Acts of 1871 and 1875 which permitted strikes and picketing. The Trades Union Congress (TUC) had been formed in 1868 and by the 1880s, therefore, Britain had a flourishing union movement with well over one million members. Then, with the growth of socialism, union history began an important change.

The Labour Party

The 1880s witnessed the birth of what has been called a 'new unionism'. Influenced by the ideas of the German socialist philosopher, Karl Marx (1818–1883), union leaders believed that the only really effective way to help their members was to destroy the capitalist industrial system. Unskilled workers were recruited in their thousands. Strikes became more common and the successful London Dock Strike of August, 1889 played an important part in the rise of this new unionism.

While the trade union movement was growing, another group of socialists, led by the Scotsman Keir Hardie (1856–1915), had formed a new political party. It was known as the Independent Labour Party. In 1888 Hardie was elected as its

Keir Hardie addressing a gathering of the Independent Labour Party in Trafalgar Square, London. Hardie was elected as its first MP in 1888.

first MP. The ILP realized, however, that they had to have union support if they were ever to become a real political force; by 1900 union funds amounted to almost £4 million.

During the 1890s the Trades Union Congress, many of whose members were not socialists, was won round to Hardie's point of view. It was worried by the uncertain economic conditions and the way employers were organizing themselves to take on the unions. Therefore, in February 1900 a Labour Representation Committee was formed with the support of the TUC. Its aim was to get representatives of the working class elected to Parliament. Very soon it was known simply as the Labour Party.

Today the trade unions and the Labour Party remain closely linked. The unions provide the party with the bulk of its funds and have a majority say in the choice of party leader.

Today the trade unions provide the Labour Party with most of its funds which help finance events such as the annual conference.

Trade Unions this Century

The trade unions have been the most successful interest group of the twentieth century. In the years before the First World War they persuaded the Liberal government to pass two Acts (1906 and 1913) which freed them to call strikes and enabled them to use their funds for political purposes. Widespread industrial action won lower hours of work in several industries and higher wages in others. During the war the unions formed a 'Treasury Agreement' with the government, not to disrupt the war effort.

Between the First and Second World Wars the unions had only mixed success. The period saw Britain's first two Labour governments (1924 and 1929–31) and a General Strike (1926). Nevertheless, the poor state of Britain's economy and the unfavourable attitude of a series of Conservative Prime Ministers ensured that union pressure for

Between the two World Wars the unions had mixed success. These Manchester tramwaymen are on a protest march during the General Strike of 1926.

the improvement of the working and living conditions of their members had only limited effect.

The years 1945–1979 saw the trade union movement at the height of its power. Hours of work were reduced, people were made more secure in their jobs, and wages rose. But gradually the feeling grew amongst some politicians that, despite the good they did, the unions were so powerful that they presented a threat to the effective working of Britain's representative democracy.

In 1945 union membership totalled 7,875,000; by 1977 it had risen to 12,701,000. Edward Heath's Conservative government, which had promised to reform union power, was itself brought down by union action in 1974. Then, following failure to reach an agreed limit to wage rises, a Labour government was faced with a series of strikes during the 1978–9 'winter of discontent'. The Conservatives, who were pledged once more to curb union power, won the subsequent general election of May, 1979.

The dustmen's strike was one of many during the 1978–79 'winter of discontent'. Scenes like this were common at the time.

The Unions Today

Margaret Thatcher came to office in 1979 determined to reduce trade union power. She believed that the unions were not only undermining the government's authority, but also preventing the working of a free economy. Mrs Thatcher wanted wages and prices to find a 'natural' level, without government interference or what she saw as excessive union demands.

The Conservatives struck at the unions in two ways. Firstly, they passed laws to regulate union activity. Ballots had to be held before strike action could be taken, picketing was curbed and unions' political contributions were also subjected to a ballot. Staff at the Government Communications Headquarters in Cheltenham were not allowed union membership.

The second part of the attack on the unions involved not discussing economic policy with

Margaret Thatcher, shortly after the announcement of her victory in the general election of May, 1979. Part of the Conservative election campaign was a pledge to reduce trade union power.

The high unemployment of the 1980s has resulted in a decline in union membership.

them, and refusing to intervene directly in strikes. When faced with a major strike previous governments had often invited the two sides to come together to find a compromise. Mrs Thatcher refused to do this, preferring to let strikes run their course.

The clearest example of this was the prolonged miners' strike of 1984–5, which ended in defeat for the National Union of Mineworkers and a split in the union. The massive unemployment of the 1980s undermined union authority. By 1986 union membership had fallen by a quarter in seven years.

People will argue for years to come about the rights and wrongs of the Conservative government's treatment of the unions. Whatever one feels, however, it should not be forgotten that over the century they have done more than any other group to further the welfare of the great majority of British people.

Interest Groups

The CBI (Confederation of British Industry) is a powerful interest group consisting of all the major employers. Like the political parties it holds an annual conference to discuss policies.

As we have seen, pressure groups can be divided into 'interest' and 'cause' groups. The former, of whom the trade unions are by far the best-known example, seek to promote the welfare of their members, all of whom share a major common interest. In the case of a union, this common interest is their employment. For example, in the 1980s British Rail had to face long and sometimes bitter opposition from the rail unions over its proposal to introduce 'driver only' trains: the unions feared that this move would lead to fewer jobs in the industry and possible redundancy.

Apart from the trade unions, there are three other broad categories of interest group. Business groups are the most powerful. The leading organization is the Confederation of British Industry (CBI) which has a large and well-financed structure, not unlike that of the TUC, which keeps an eye on government departments and is always on hand to put forward the views of employers.

Another type of interest group is the professional association. This exists to safeguard the interests of a highly-qualified group of workers. Doctors join the British Medical Association, and teachers join groups such as the National Union of Teachers, or the Assistant Masters and Mistresses Association. It is worth noting that some professional groups are also unions, showing how difficult the categorization of pressure groups is.

Finally, there are numerous miscellaneous interest groups, covering areas such as recreation, religion or travel. For example the MCC (Marylebone Cricket Club), the Buddhist Society and motorist's associations like the RAC (Royal Automobile Club) and the AA (Automobile Association). Through such organizations a large proportion of the population is involved in pressure group activity.

The NUT (National Union of Teachers) is an interest group which is a trade union and a professional association. These teachers are demonstrating for more pay.

Cause Groups

Cause groups exist to put forward a single objective. This can be very specific: as for example, the campaign to discourage smoking (ASH), or the Campaign for Nuclear Disarmament. Other groups have more general causes. The British Association for the Advancement of Science aims to increase public awareness of science, ensure that more science is taught in schools and to improve the standard of science teaching.

By their very nature, interest groups are open to a limited range of people. Only car-owners belong to the RAC, only teachers to the NUT. Cause groups, on the other hand, appeal to a wide cross-section of the population. Members of the

The British Association for the Advancement of Science is a cause group which strives to improve the standard of science teaching in schools.

Members of a group can draw attention to their cause by organizing a protest march. Over 100,000 people joined this CND (Campaign for Nuclear Disarmament) march through London in 1981.

Campaign for the Protection of Rural England (CPRE) are both men and women, town and country dwellers, from all walks of life in all parts of the country. All they have in common is a wish to see the beauties of rural Britain preserved from industrial, urban and farm development.

Another difference between cause and interest groups is the amount of notice taken of them by the government and political parties. The large interest groups can afford to pay MPs to represent them in Parliament: of the 269 Labour MPs elected in 1979, 133 were sponsored by trade unions. Cause groups are rarely wealthy enough to do this, and they have to rely more on outside pressure to promote their cause.

Pressure Groups in Action

There is a wide variety of ways in which a pressure group can draw attention to its cause. For trade unions the obvious weapon is the strike. Business groups, particularly multinationals, can lock out workers, move their business or even – in the case of an international company – threaten to leave the country altogether. These tactics do not get much publicity but they can put considerable pressure on a government.

All pressure groups, both cause and interest, at some time or other run publicity campaigns. They use posters, leaflets, books, and advertisements on television and radio. The Live Aid

Pressure groups use all sorts of publicity material including books, leaflets, posters and banners. NUPE stands for National Union of Public Employees.

campaign, which raised money for famine victims in Africa, was one of the most successful pressure group campaigns of recent years. Cause groups are particularly keen to be filmed by the television cameras. To do this they will stage protests to draw attention to themselves. The women members of CND who camped outside the American air base of Greenham Common and obstructed the activity of the base obtained widespread media coverage.

The two key targets for pressure group activity are Parliament (dealt with in the next chapter) and the Civil Service. The routine government of the country is in the hands of civil servants at Whitehall, and even when changes in policy are made MPs have to rely heavily on civil servants for advice. Thus, pressure groups need to influence civil servants as much as MPs.

The pressure groups who have the most influence in Whitehall are usually those who have advice and expertise to offer the civil servants. This is given through advisory committees. The Ministry of Agriculture and Fisheries, for example, relies heavily on the co-operation of the National Farmers' Union, without whom, it is said, agricultural policy could not be provided.

Above left *Nearly 80,000 people attended the Live Aid Concert on 13 July, 1985 at Wembley Stadium in London.* **Above right** *The singer Bob Geldof master-minded the campaign to raise money for famine victims in Africa.*

Pressure on Parliament

Parliament lies at the heart of the British political system, and so it is here that pressure groups focus their attention. The traditional place for Members of Parliament to meet with members of the public is in one of the lobbies in the Palace of Westminster. These are broad rooms between the Palace's passages and corridors. The word 'lobby' now has another meaning: to seek to influence an MP to help one's cause.

One of the best ways for a group to ensure that its voice is heard in Parliament is to pay an MP a fee to watch over its interests. More than 100 MPs are consultants to private companies, and many work for unions and other groups. There are also at least thirty full-time lobbyists, men and women who can be employed to lobby MPs.

Fishermen from all over Britain gathering outside Westminster for a mass lobby of Parliament in February, 1982. This is the traditional way for a pressure group to influence Parliament.

MPs are often grateful to the lobby groups for the information they provide. But the growth of lobbying in recent years has given cause for concern. MPs are bombarded with letters, offered meals and even holidays abroad to persuade them to use their influence on behalf of some group or other. The worry is that there is no register of lobbyists in which groups can state clearly what they are doing and who they are paying. Sometimes, therefore, because it is secret, the influence of the lobby can appear corrupt.

The traditional way for a pressure group to influence Parliament is to organize a demonstration, or a mass lobby. Hundreds of supporters assemble outside the Palace of Westminster, often singing and waving placards. Sometimes huge petitions, bearing thousands of signatures, are presented to Parliament or to individual ministers.

A petition with 134,845 signatures protesting against Sunday trading being delivered to 10, Downing Street in December 1982.

The Need for Pressure Groups

Pressure groups play a vital part in our democracy. One of their functions is to link the government with the people between elections. In countries where unions and pressure groups do not exist, unless the government works hard to listen to people's views, it can find itself introducing unpopular policies and becoming insensitive to the needs of ordinary citizens.

A second important function of pressure groups is to provide the government and MPs with information. For example, while he was working on reform of the law on abortion, the MP John Corrie received considerable help from the Society for the Protection of the Unborn Child. Without them, he said, 'I simply could not have done the work myself.' Help like this makes our democracy more efficient.

Pressure groups look after the interests of minorities – prisoners are represented by the organization known as PROP (Preservation of the Rights of Prisoners).

These young people are helping with conservation work for the National Trust. Through this work they are involving themselves with a group which has political influence.

Another argument frequently put forward in favour of pressure groups is that they look after the interests of minority groups. Although the major British political parties contain representatives of a wide range of viewpoints, they tend to favour the opinions which will bring them the most votes. There is little incentive, for example, for them to give much time to prisoners' matters. Pressure groups like PROP (Preservation of the Rights of Prisoners) undertake this task.

Finally, pressure groups involve people in politics who otherwise might not feel concerned with political matters. Through membership of the National Trust someone who shows little interest in party politics throws their weight behind a group with political power. In this way pressure groups help to maintain the vigour of our democratic government.

Lobbying in a Democracy

Pressure groups are not without their critics. In recent years pressure group activity has increased considerably, causing concern at the political power being exerted by these private organizations. Mrs Thatcher's Conservative government went some way to curbing union power, when it seemed to rival that of the elected government. But other groups, such as the CBI, continue to wield massive influence.

One problem with pressure group influence is that it is often used in secret. We are told of government decisions, such as the decision to build a power station on a particular site, but we do not know how or why the decision was reached. A Conservative government, for example, might be influenced by the offer of a contribution to party funds from a manufacturer of generators,

Doctors can lobby effectively for their interests through their professional organization, the British Medical Association.

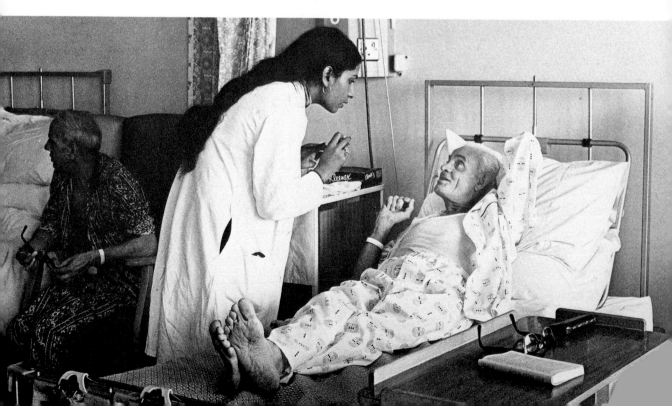

while a Labour government could find themselves under similar pressure from a wealthy union such as the NUM.

Pressure groups, despite the considerable influence they exert in our democracy, are not themselves necessarily democratically organized. Leaders are usually appointed, not elected, and members are rarely consulted over policy. Moreover, already privileged sections of the community, like doctors and lawyers, lobby effectively for their interests. Weaker groups, such as pensioners, form less influential groups. Thus pressure groups can increase existing inequalities.

In a free society it is not easy to see how pressure groups can be kept working for democracy rather than against it. First steps might include a compulsory register of all lobby activity at Westminster, and a Freedom of Information Act. This would allow the public more access to the workings of government, enabling them to see more clearly how decisions were being made on their behalf.

Less influential sections of the community like pensioners have to work particularly hard to protect their interests.

Protest

The suffragettes were a protest group who were campaigning to obtain the vote for women before the First World War.

On the fringe of pressure groups are protest groups. These are not political parties, yet they differ from pressure groups in their aims and tactics. They are often disillusioned with conventional politics and want to change the attitudes of society as a whole, although their ideas are not always carefully thought through. Protest groups can be found attached to many causes, including CND, anti-vivisection, anti-apartheid and women's rights.

The activities of protest groups sometimes bring them into conflict with the law. Some groups hold demonstrations in public places, often blocking roads and causing inconvenience. One of the most famous protest groups was the suffragettes, campaigning at the start of this century for votes for women. Their efforts were rewarded when the Representation of the Peoples Act, was passed in

February, 1918. This gave the vote to a limited number of women; but full electoral equality did not come until 1928.

The theory behind protest groups is twofold. They believe that ordinary pressure group tactics will not bring about the changes they seek. Secondly, by creating as big a nuisance as possible they hope to draw attention to their cause.

Because dramatic events such as riots never fail to gain media coverage, these protest groups and their causes do get brought to the attention of the public. Occasionally the activities of more extreme pressure groups actually endanger people's lives. As long as our government is open and fair, and the legitimate activities of pressure groups can be seen to have effect, there is really no necessity for violence.

Protest groups support causes such as animal rights, anti-apartheid and women's rights.

Important Dates

1824	Combination Acts repealed, leading to increased trade union activity; Royal Society for the Prevention of Cruelty to Animals founded.
1834	Robert Owen's Grand National Consolidated Trade Union founded.
1838–46	Anti-Corn Law League's successful reform campaign.
1851	'Tolpuddle Martyrs' transported for forming a union. Amalgamated Society of Engineers founded.
1868	First Trades Union Congress.
1871	Acts legalized trade unions.
1875	Strikes and picketing given legal protection.
1889	London dock strike.
1897	RAC founded.
1900	Labour Party founded.
1901	Taff Vale case threatened unions' right to call strikes.
1906	Trades Disputes Act reversed Taff Vale judgement.
1914	Triple Alliance of miners, railwaymen and transport workers formed.
1926	General Strike.
1927	Union activity curbed by legislation.
1946	First majority Labour government repealed legislation of 1927.
1956	Aldermaston march of CND.
1965	CBI set up.
1966	Shelter (National Campaign for the Homeless) founded.
1971	Industrial Relations Act to limit union power.
1972	Massive wave of strikes.
1974	Labour government established 'Social Contract' with unions.
1978–9	'Winter of discontent'.
1980–4	Series of Acts limited union power.
1984–5	Miners' strike.

Further Reading

Alderman, G., *Pressure Groups and Government in Britain* (Longman, 1984)

Coxall, W. N., *Parties and Pressure Groups* (Longman, 1981)

Field, F., *Poverty and Politics* (Heinemann, 1982)

May, R., *Pressure Groups* (Wayland, 1983)

Pelling, H., *A History of British Trade Unionism* (Penguin, 1969)

Silverman, N., *Trade Unions* (Wayland, 1983)

Taylor, R., *The Fifth Estate: Britain's Unions in the Modern World* (Pan, 1980)

Glossary

Act   A law passed by Parliament.

Ballots   Votes, usually written down in secret.

Capitalism   An economic system based on the private ownership of the means of production.

Civil Service   The branches of government which are not elected.

Constituency   A district in the United Kingdom represented by an MP in the House of Commons.

Constituent   A resident of a constituency, especially one entitled to vote.

Curb   Restrain.

Democracy   Government with the consent of the people.

Demonstration   A public protest meeting, sometimes taking the form of a rally or parade.

Disarmament   Reduction in the number of weapons a country possesses.

EEC   The European Economic Community or Common Market.

Economy   The whole of a country's resources.

General election   The election by which MPs are chosen for the House of Commons.

General strike   A strike of all workers.

Industrial action   Any action, such as a strike or go-slow, taken by employees in industry to protest against working conditions.

MP   A Member of Parliament. A person who has been elected to voice the wishes of his or her local community in Parliament.

Multinational   Operating in several countries.

Media   Television, radio and the press.

Opinion poll   A questionnaire to discover people's views.

Petition   A written protest or request.

Policy   The intentions of a political group.

Radical   Wanting deep-rooted change.

Redundancy   State or condition of being redundant.

Redundant   Deprived of one's job because it is no longer necessary for efficient operation.

Socialist   Advocating the ownership of commerical activity by the state.

Sponsor   Support with money.

Strike   To withdraw labour; refuse to work.

Trade union   A group of workers from the same field of employment, organized to further its interests in such areas as pay and working conditions.

TUC   The Trades Union Congress.

Westminster   The House of Parliament at Westminster.

Whitehall   The Civil Service in London.

Index

Acknowledgements

The illustrations in this book were supplied by: Camera Press Limited 16, 8, 27; ET Archives 28; Sally and Richard Greenhill 26; National Trust 25; Popperfoto 10, 14, 19; Rex Features Limited cover, 13, 17; Frank Spooner Pictures 20, 21; Syndication International 24; Topham Picture Library 5, 6, 7, 9, 11, 15, 22, 23, 29; Wayland Picture Library 8, 12; Zefa 4.